# What We Said, What We Heard, and Why It Matters

## A Report of the Together Conversations

by Steve Clapp

Brethren Press

What We Said, What We Heard, and Why It Matters
A Report of the Together Conversations
Steve Clapp

Book design: The Concept Mill
Together logo design: Debbie Noffsinger

ISBN: 978-0-87178-104-8


12  11  10  09  08        1  2  3  4  5

Printed in the United States of America

# Contents

# Together

"Together" has been a national emphasis in the Church of the Brethren to encourage people to think and talk about what it means to be the church. What the church is and does is shaped by our everyday words and actions as people of faith. But periodically it's worth taking time to study and talk about these understandings. The last time the Church of the Brethren engaged in such a study was fifty years ago, close to the 250th anniversary of the denomination. This time, on the eve of our 300th anniversary, the hope has been to involve as many people as possible in the conversation.

**Together has given us opportunity to grow in the maturity of our faith and in our understanding of what God calls us to be and to do.**

The Together emphasis had no required outcome, no detailed objectives, no policies to be voted on, and no decisions to be made. Rather, this time together has been about asking what God's yearning is for us as a church. Together has given us opportunity to grow in the maturity of our faith and in our understanding of what God calls us to be and to do.

# The process

The original concept of a conversation about the nature of the church was developed in a meeting of the district executives of the denomination. They then sought to involve others in the project, and a planning committee worked for years to develop the process for a series of conversations. Those involved in that planning include the Council of District Executives and the agencies of the Church of the Brethren— the Association of Brethren Caregivers, Bethany Theological Seminary, Brethren Benefit Trust, the General Board, and On Earth Peace— as well as the officers of Annual Conference.

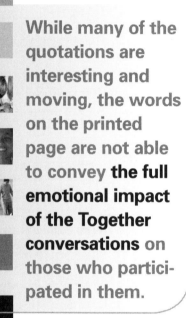

**While many of the quotations are interesting and moving, the words on the printed page are not able to convey the full emotional impact of the Together conversations on those who participated in them.**

The official launch of Together was at a gathering in New Windsor, Maryland, in February 2006. Together conversations have taken place in a variety of settings across the church:

- There were Together conversations at Annual Conference in 2006.

- The districts have held Together conversations at district conferences and in other district settings. Trained

"Listening Teams" have made careful notes on the topics, themes, and examples shared in those district events.

- Significant Together conversations also took place at the National Older Adult Conference (NOAC) and at National Youth Conference (NYC). Notes were made of the literally thousands of comments by people participating in those national events.

- Groups such as district clergy, the On Earth Peace board, and other organizations have held Together conversations. A report was submitted from the Church of the Brethren in Brazil.

Many congregations used *Together: Conversations on Being the Church*, the conversation guide written by Jim

Benedict. The hope was to have all the congregations in the denomination take part in this conversation, and all congregations were asked to share a summary of their thoughts. While not every congregation shared a report, many did so. This overview shares observations based on the notes from the launch event, on reports from the Listening Teams in the districts, on the NOAC and NYC conversations, on the summaries provided by congregations that have completed the Together process, and on notes from other groups that participated in the process.

It's important to remember that the primary purpose of the Together conversations was to engage people across the denomination in talking about the nature of the church. The Together initiative was not designed to provide the kind of sociological look at the church that Carl Bowman offers in *Portrait of a People,* a report of the Brethren Member Profile 2006. It was also not designed to produce data to assess congregational health, like the Congregational Survey process of Christian Community and New Life Ministries.

The greatest consistency in reporting came from the work of the Listening Teams in the districts. The feedback from individual churches participating in Together conversations ranged from as brief a report as a single line about the nature of the church to a fifteen-page document. The responses from all those reporting came in narrative form rather than objective form. When data come in objective form, it is possible to readily say that a certain percentage of people have had a certain experience or feel a certain way about the church. Information that comes in narrative reports is generally more interesting to read, but difficult to quantify.

Having given those qualifications, it's still very important for us to consider some observations that clearly emerge from the Together process. Almost every church in the denomination had at least one person who took part in Together conversations in at least one setting: Annual Conference, district meetings, NYC, NOAC, or the local church. Some congregations had virtually every active member participate in the study and conversation held in their local church.

Attendance counts were not provided with every report that was submitted, but it's likely that around 20,000 persons were a part of the conversations on which those reports were based. And it is impossible to estimate the number who took part in Together conversations for which no report was submitted. It will probably be a long time before there is another effort that generates so much discussion about the nature of the church.

The Together steering team engaged the services of Christian Community, Inc., to process the reports that were received. Christian Community has conducted many national studies and has considerable experience in working with both

**The church at its best has tremendous room for impact on the lives of people in our often troubled world.**

quantitative and qualitative data. Computer programs were used to examine the reports for key words and phrases. Three trained people read through every single report to identify trends and themes. This report pulls together the observations from that process.

Where possible, the decision has been to let the story of the Together process be told in the words of those who were part of it. You'll find many quotations in this overview. They've been chosen either because of their insightfulness or because of their being representative of what dozens or even hundreds of others said.

While many of the quotations are interesting and moving, the words on the printed page are not able to convey the full emotional impact of the Together conversations on those who participated in them. The Listening Teams who attended the district events shared accounts of conversations that were really transforming, with people from different backgrounds and different perspectives finding themselves with deeper understandings of one another. The sharing of memories and hopes in many congregational settings brought new insights and energy to those who participated.

**What is the nature of the church?** The Together conversations invited people to share in exploring that theme and to talk about **God's yearning for the Church of the Brethren.**

No written report can capture the essence of those experiences. The best way to grasp the original impact may be to share with others in talking about this overview. A discussion guide has been provided at the end of the overview to encourage conversations in group settings.

# Salad oil and the church

A group of Church of the Brethren clergy shared a meal at a Golden Corral restaurant. Their waitress told them that a friend, another waitress, was about to have a biopsy for suspected cancer and was distraught about it. She asked them if they would pray for her friend, and of course they said they would be glad to do so.

The friend was working at the restaurant at that time, and she joined the ministers at their table. They used a bit of salad oil from the table and anointed the woman for healing in the middle of the Golden Corral! Follow-up calls were made by one of the pastors, and the waitress, at last report, was doing well.

The church at its best has tremendous room for impact on the lives of people in our often troubled world. This group of clergy used the salad oil that was at hand to administer an ordinance that had significant meaning for the woman who received it, as well as for themselves. It likely also made an impression on others who were seated near them in the restaurant.

What is the nature of the church? The Together conversations invited people to share in exploring that theme and to talk about God's yearning for the Church of the Brethren. Here are some of the statements about the church that were made as part of the process, starting with the most concise response:

- The church is a caring, fun, nice, friendly, awesome family for anybody.

- God's yearning for the Church of the Brethren is that we be a community which glorifies him and a fellowship of believers with emphasis on New Testament teaching with an attitude of service and peace, as well as a mission to reach out and evangelize. As a community of believers, we strive to be open to God's guidance in our worship and Bible study, seeking unity, peace, and selflessness by accepting and caring for one another within the community of faith.

- *Simplest version:* Our goal: to know Him. Our mission: to make Him known.

  *Simple version:* Disciples making other disciples, in authentic community, for the glory of God and the good of the world.

  *More defined version:* Doing the Word by passionately modeling the life of Christ, we seek to be a growing community through significant relationships with seekers as well as believers, caring holistically for the needs of others. As a ministering church, we will, as "wounded healers," demonstrate the relevance of Christ by using his resources and our experiences.

- As a messenger to the whole world, we encourage individuals from all walks of life to attend and participate in the life and activities of our church. Additionally, we trust that the Holy Spirit will always be at work in the lives of those who seek Him, to convict us of our sins and to encourage us to live lives consistent with the Word of God. Therefore, although we will not affirm a lifestyle choice that clearly is in contrast to biblical teachings, we do desire to welcome everyone and anyone into our church.

**We are called to welcome everyone without exception, to provide a loving community of faith, and to equip one another for ministry in the world. We are called to spread the good news of Jesus Christ....**

- God is yearning for Jesus to be at the center of our faith and life as it was at the beginning of the Church of the Brethren. God is yearning for every church to be united in living as we state in our bulletin each Sunday: "As a Christian community, striving to be peacemakers, we are called by Christ to be inclusive and caring. We affirm that people of any race, ethnic identity, gender, sexual orientation, economic status, education level, ability, age, or life situation are welcome in our congregation."

- The church is called to be as a "light on a hill," proclaiming Jesus as Lord and Savior. The church is the people of God doing the work of Jesus, through service, encouragement, involvement, uniting in love and forgiving one another. God yearns for us to be more loving, less critical of differences of opinion, and "one in the bond of love," led by the Holy Spirit.

- We believe the key to becoming more like the church God yearns for us to be is to look at what was originally established and use that for a model. Unfortunately, the more popular trend is to try and make the church more attractive to the world by becoming more like the world, which is in direct violation of God's word. We need to stress that intolerance to sin is not mean-spirited and close-minded, but is driven by a desire to do that which is right and pleasing to Jesus Christ. And what pleases him the most is being obedient to his call to evangelize the world so

**Together participants talked often about the importance of the acceptance and the caring that they have experienced within their local congregations.**

that none should be lost. To summarize, it is not so much what we need to become but what we should return to.

- To become more like the church God yearns for us to be, we need:
  - Healing of woundedness
  - Greater reliance on faith
  - Unconditional love
  - Greater acceptance of everyone
  - Vibrant community of justice and joy
  - Continued existence and growth
  - To be less afraid
  - To limit critical spirits
  - To value and enjoy diversity
  - To act on a terrific sense of mission
  - To seek God.

- Collectively and individually, Brethren need to be the Lord's disciples, using Jesus as their example and the New Testament as their guide. Accept variety, live simply, and be good stewards of the environment and of all the gifts God bestows. Love one another, show compassion for those in need, reach out and make disciples, and welcome the stranger in our midst. Support one another in the faith through worship, fellowship, and sharing of joys and concerns. Walk humbly and be constant in faith. Nurture life in Christ through prayer, meditation, and Bible study. Practice the ordinances. Work for justice, peace, and reconciliation. Learn to forgive. Wait patiently on the Lord. Seek God's will.

• We are called to welcome everyone without exception, to provide a loving community of faith, and to equip one another for ministry in the world. We are called to spread the good news of Jesus Christ through talking about our faith, inviting others to church, working for justice, and striving for peace. We celebrate our heritage, rejoice at God's work in the present, and move with confidence into the future— knowing that God will guide us if our hearts and minds are open.

# Observations

1 **Together participants talked often about the importance of the acceptance and the caring that they have experienced within their local congregations.** That acceptance and caring have indeed been life-transforming for many persons. Some of the strongest affirmations of this care came from teenagers participating in the National Youth Conference. The first three quotations are from youth.

• When I had surgery, the whole youth group came to the

hospital to see me. I received cards from people I didn't even know. The Church of the Brethren really cares.

- The church is like my home. It's where I belong. It's where everybody cares about you and about what happens to you.

- I feel the presence of Jesus when I'm with people in my church. People care about each other, and they'll do anything for someone in need.

- We come from settings, both personal and work, where acceptance is lacking. If we don't find affirmation in the church, then we're really in bad shape. More and more people are coming from situations of brokenness. The church says that you are of value because you are a child of God.

- When I went through divorce, I did a great job of condemning myself. I was desperate for a real sense of forgiveness and acceptance. The church gave that to me and changed my life.

- When my mother died, the people of the church absolutely embraced me with their love. The loss was so enormous that I would never have made it without all that love and encouragement.

- I came to the Church of the Brethren from a church that was a lot more judgmental, that demanded you agree with certain beliefs. I was amazed and delighted to find out that the Church of the Brethren has a much broader umbrella and encourages people to work out their own theology rather than relying on a creed. And the love and acceptance of people has just been overwhelming.

- I got involved in the church because my son started attending a mid-week supper and study. I saw what a difference the church made in his life, and I wanted to experience the same thing. The spirit of Christ is alive in this congregation.

- I have a fairly serious mental illness, and I've always been reluctant to become involved in a church. I just have too much wrong with me. I started going to this particular congregation because my therapist told me it was a safe place. He was really telling the truth. I've found so much love and acceptance here. It's truly helped me become a healthier person.

- An elderly neighbor invited us to start coming to the church. I'd been hurt in another congregation and was very reluctant to come. I've been amazed by the love of people, and I started getting involved in a service project at the church. Working with the other people has transformed my life, and it's also transformed the life of my children.

- I've been in the same church virtually all of my life, from the time my parents moved to this community when I was eight years old. I'm 83 now, so you can see I've been here awhile. My best friends are in this church, and the church has been with me through some of the most joyous and tragic times of my life. I experience the living presence of Jesus in this congregation. And while I don't know all the new people who've been joining the church in recent years, I can see that many of them are finding the same rewards here that I have.

**The emphasis on service was lifted up with appreciation in many of the Together conversations. People who differ with one another on some theological issues come together to serve others as Christ taught us to do.**

2 **As valuable as those feelings and experiences are for most of those whose views were reported,** it's important to remember that not everyone has experienced that same caring. Some people shared disappointment. For example:

- I brought a friend of mine from high school to our church, and I was really disappointed. My friend looks a little rough. He has long hair and some piercings and a tattoo. I guess he and I look a lot different. But he's this really gentle, kind person. People just didn't respond well to him. They stared at him, and a couple of people actually said things to him that hurt his feelings. I'll not make the mistake of inviting someone to our church again.

- I like our church, and the peace emphasis is so important to me. But I've been a member for a decade now, and I still feel like a second-class citizen because I didn't grow up in the denomination, and I don't have a "Brethren name." People in our church just don't see you as having the same value if you came from another denomination and if you aren't related to someone they know. I don't know how we can ever grow as a denomination if other churches are like this one.

- I stopped attending church for over six months when we were going through some difficult times in my home. I'm back now, and it feels good. But in that whole time I was gone, not one person in the church called or stopped by to see if anything was wrong. Wouldn't you think that someone would want to find out if you were having problems or if you had been hurt by something that happened at church? I don't feel the same way about this church that I did before, but I'm trying to hang in and make things better.

- When our son came out as homosexual, I was disappointed in the response of our church. People were so judgmental about it. The thing is, he didn't choose to be gay. That was the last thing he wanted to have to deal with. I think that's why he got engaged and almost got married; he was fighting it. But it just turns out that he is gay. He can't help it, and I think that's the way God made him. People are so quick to judge and on the basis of just a few biblical passages. I don't think people genuinely cared about us or our son, or they would have tried harder to understand.

- I've made myself unpopular in my church because I feel like there are some lines that have to be drawn. Divorce is a sin. Homosexuality is a sin. You can feel sorry for the people who go through a divorce, and you can feel sorry for people who are homosexual. But I think the Scriptures are clear. Well, a lot of people in my church don't feel that way, and they've made it clear that they don't appreciate my point of view.

3 **Together participants have strongly affirmed many of the traditional practices and values of the Church of the Brethren.** Love feast, the ordinance of anointing, service, and the commitment to peace have been repeatedly emphasized in conversations at NOAC, at NYC, in districts, and in local congregations. Consider these comments:

- When we attended love feast for the first time in our church, well, words can't describe what I experienced— candlelight in the old fellowship hall, in tight quarters, the intimacy of the service, it was a spiritual high. Love feast is such a powerful image of the church.

- After September 11, 2001, my heart was filled with rage at the people who had attacked us. Then our church had a special prayer service and offered anointing to any who wanted it. When the oil went on my forehead, I felt the anger and frustration and pain lifted right out of me by the power of God.

- When I was in the hospital with cancer, facing a second surgery, my minister and two other people from the church came to anoint me. It was the most uplifting experience of my life. They didn't make any extravagant promises about what the anointing would do for me; but after they did it, I could feel this burden rolling off of me. I knew that God was going to be with me through whatever came. I've been cancer-free for three years now, and I give praise to God for it.

The emphasis on service was lifted up with appreciation in many of the Together conversations. People who differ with one another on some theological issues come together to serve others as Christ taught us to do. Here are a few of the statements that were shared:

- I've always looked up to the three people in our church who were in BVS (Brethren Volunteer Service). I'm looking forward to doing that myself when I'm old enough.

- Our church is at its best in responding to disasters, wherever they happen to be. We send money, and we send people. It shows how very alive our faith is.

- Heifer Project has made a difference in the lives of people all around the world. So many denominations participate in it now, that I think a lot of people don't even realize that it started in the Church of the Brethren.

- People in our church really turn out to help build Habitat for Humanity homes. We do it as community projects, but our church provides at least half the people.

- I like belonging to a denomination that shows such compassion for those in the middle of disasters. We respond, and we respond quickly.

- No one can accurately measure the impact of BVS on people in our denomination and on the people who've been served through that program. It's one of the best things about being Brethren.

- I know that we're not supposed to be prideful, but it's hard not to feel pride about the way our denomination responds when there's a disaster. We respond as well as some denominations that are ten or twenty times our size.

- It's great that our denomination has programs like Heifer Project and BVS. The other thing that is great at the level of our local church is how quickly people respond when there is a need in the church or the

**Being a peace church is central to the identity of many of the congregations** that responded, but there are some that did not mention the topic in their responses and others that seem to equate a strong stance for peace as being unsupportive of people in the military.

community. We just finished repainting the home of an elderly woman who has little money. We provide meals and childcare for people in a health crisis. Whatever the need, our church responds. That's true for many, maybe most, of the churches in the denomination.

The strongest statements about the peace position of the denomination were made by participants at NYC and at NOAC. Young people are especially pleased to be in a church that places so much value on peace.

While most of the comments about the peace emphasis of the denomination were extremely positive, there were a few exceptions. Reports from congregations were not as likely to emphasize the importance of work for peace as were reports from regional (district) and national gatherings.

There also appear to be some differing opinions on what it means to be a peace church, though that is a core part of our heritage. Being a peace church is central to the identity of many of the congregations that responded, but there are some that did not mention the topic in their responses and others that seem to equate a strong stance for peace as being unsupportive of people in the military. Yet there are also churches that consider the peace position to be very important and yet have active members in the military. Consider these comments:

- Lots of churches are in favor of peace when life is calm. The thing about the Church of the Brethren is that we are always a peace church, even when it isn't popular. Almost everyone now says that the war in Iraq is a mess and that we should probably never have gone there. I'm pleased that my pastor and local church took that position before it was popular.

- Our congregation has a Congressional Medal of Honor recipient.

- I've been in the National Guard for twenty years, and I've been a committed member of the Church of the Brethren that whole time. I feel called to the military, but I also feel called to work for peace. I'm thankful that my local church has accepted me and affirmed me even when my approach to peace was different than that of some others.

- Pacifism is an insidious infection that has crept into the denomination, a subtle anti-Americanism.

- People in our church feel caught. We believe we are called to be peace-makers, and we respect that part of our tradition.

**People also expressed their concerns and their hopes about the state of the church today and about the future.**

Yet some of us have loved ones who are in the military, and we don't want to come across as disrespectful of them.

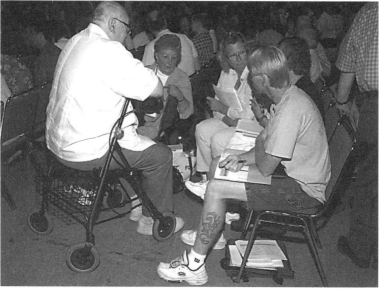

- I was proud of our denomination when our general secretary made such a bold statement against our going to war in Iraq. People were waving the flag in lots of other churches, but our denomination has the courage to say what's right and what's wrong. And I don't see how war can ever be right.

- We have a responsibility to our young people to educate them about the peace position of our church. We may not have a draft now, but we will again sometime. And there are young people who enlist in the military without thinking about what they are doing. I'm not saying that it's always wrong for someone to be in the military, but it needs to be a thoughtful decision.

- I feel so good about being a part of the Church of the Brethren and taking such a strong stand for peace. You can tell that faith makes a difference in the lives of people in our church. It feels good to work for peace, to strive to make a difference.

# 4 Several talked about changes that have happened within congregations and within the denomination.

Some shared warm memories of the way things were done in the past accompanied by a certain regret over the changes that have occurred. Listening Team members shared the observation that some of those comments reflected nostalgia and some reflected grief. Nostalgia carries the hope that something from the past can be recovered in the future. Grief mourns the passing of something that will not be recovered, but grief also allows something new to come into being.

**The topics of biblical interpretation and homosexuality** were the ones over which differences of opinion were most apparent.

Some elements of the past are clearly part of our roots and need to be preserved, though the outward form may change to connect with new generations. Other elements of the past, while very meaningful, may not be as essential a part of our roots. Individual Christians, congregations, and the denomination have the challenge of assessing what the true roots of our faith and tradition are.

The statements that came from participants in the National Older Adult Conference (NOAC) were, for the most part, very affirming of changes that have happened. Years of living appear to give many a healthy perspective on the way that change is a part of life. Here are some comments from older adults reflecting an awareness that we have gone through significant changes in the past and will in the future:

- Think of the rules that we once had that we don't even think about anymore. . . . If you were baptized in another church, your baptism was accepted only if you were baptized in flowing water. You were not allowed to shave certain ways. There were no Sunday schools originally.

- Some went ahead and went to college when that wasn't encouraged. Eventually rules and expectations changed. Now we encourage all our young people to go to college.

- We aren't going to go back to the kind of simple life that was shown in clothing and beards and head-coverings that set us apart. But we can still find ways to express the values of simple living in society today, and society needs that message.

- Although the church should maintain core values such as the love feast, the church should be open to change in traditions of how the actual service is enacted.

The comments that follow come from many sources and reflect both an awareness of the importance of change and some lamentation over changes that have or have not occurred:

- I don't think newer people in our church place the same importance on things like the love feast. Attendance seems smaller every year, and the newer people just don't come. We've tried substituting hand washing for those who are uncomfortable with foot washing, but it doesn't seem to make a difference. I'm happy to have new people in the church, but I wonder if we're losing some of our identity.

**There were several who voiced their concern about membership decline in the denomination and over the need to reach out more effectively to people who are not in the church.**

- Feet washing is awkward for our time. We're also stuck in singing the same traditional songs in the same traditional way.

- I think we are too slow to make changes in the love feast. Our church makes this meal out of canned beef on white bread, and it just isn't all that good. I know that the meal being good isn't the point of it, but why can't we do something that tastes better, especially for the teenagers? And the business of separating by male and female for the actual washing disappoints me. I'd like to sit by my husband and our children so we could wash each other's feet. I think a lot more people would be interested in coming if we made some changes. That wouldn't lose the meaning of the ordinance.

- Our worship services feel to me as though they've lost focus. We sing this modern praise music that doesn't have any depth to it. And the screen that we use is hard for a lot of us to read. I know our pastor thinks that this will help us reach younger people, but I don't see that happening in our church. We've lost something, and we've gained nothing for it.

- I want to stay in this church. It's the one I grew up in, and I love the people in it so much. But I'm disappointed that we've been slow to adapt. Our kids much prefer going to the United Methodist church just down the street where they have a praise band and use drama and videos as well as sermons. I've gone to that church with them, and I'd have to say that I like what happens there. The dramas and the videos help make the Bible come alive for life today, and I like the upbeat music. I don't know how much longer I can keep our kids coming to our church, and I don't want them to go to another church without myself and my husband.

- I think our church doesn't stay close enough to the Bible. We talk about the Bible as our rule of faith and practice, but we don't actually live that way in the church. We don't take a clear stand on things, and we aren't helping people use the Bible. We have women in the pulpit, which is clearly against Scripture; and our minister won't take a firm position against homosexuality. We've changed, and it hasn't been for the better.

- I think it's become harder and harder to deal with change. The church needs to change. I think we blow it at the national level, at the district, and in my own con-gregation because we aren't willing to change more quickly. But people are OD'd on change in their jobs, in politics, in the media. They want the church to be a place where things don't change so fast. How can we adapt to a changing culture and still offer people a safe haven? I don't have the answer.

## 5 People also expressed their concerns and their hopes about the state of the church today and about the future.
Many people are concerned about the future of the denomination and have strong feelings on some issues. The questions posed in the Together process were not necessarily designed to bring out differences of opinion, but some emerged because the issues were important to those who raised them.

The topics of biblical interpretation and homosexuality were the ones over which differences of opinion were most apparent in the Together responses. Those are also topics generating strong differences of opinion in many other denominations. Comments on these topics were more likely to come from congregations than from district events.

There were several who voiced their concern about membership decline in the denomination and over the need to reach out more effectively to people who are not in the church. A majority of the summary statements about the nature of the church included words about evangelism or outreach to those outside the church. Our continued decline, however, suggests that we are not putting those good intentions into action.

**It appears that we need to find ways for continued discussion not only of our areas of agreement but also of our areas of difference.**

Comments were also made about the authority of Annual Conference, about our denominational name, and about decisions that have been made at the denominational level.

Consider these comments of concern and hope:

• When we moved to a new Church of the Brethren, I appreciated the great music and skilled preaching. But this was a community with "named Brethren people" who saw themselves as being more important than others. I was a nobody, and that didn't feel good. What future do we have if others feel like this?

• We aren't exactly sure how to view the authority of Annual Conference. Some churches still will not accept a woman as pastor. Some churches have a more accepting view of homosexuality than the Annual Conference. Sometimes I wish Annual Conference had more authority, but I also wonder if that would tear us apart. Maybe we need to live with some ambiguity and not expect churches to act against conscience just because the Annual Conference takes a particular position.

- Most of us agree that the New Testament is our rule of faith and practice, but we don't all agree on how the Scriptures and the faith relate to some of the pressing issues of our day. How can we be respectful of one another when feelings run so strong?

- We need to recognize that the church is at times a place of conflict. Christian life is a life in relationship. . . . We won't always have harmony, and we need to show the ability to deal with conflicts and to solve them in a mature and disciplined way, but always based in the Gospel and with charity.

- We can't continue to bleed membership year after year and remain a denomination. Some of our leaders say this is just a cultural phase and that things will automatically reverse. Well, I don't see how they are going to reverse unless we become serious about planting new churches, about training people for evangelism, and about improving our hospitality.

- People of different ethnic backgrounds add so much to our congregations and our denomination. I hope we can become more multicultural in the years ahead.

- I know that people have very strong feelings about homosexuality, and I don't think there are any "bad people" in that debate. What I notice, however, because I teach high school and volunteer in the community, is that younger people are far more accepting of homosexuality that people my age. And the more I read and study, the more I think that homosexuality isn't just a choice that people are making; it's how they're made. I'm wondering if we are going to end up on the wrong side of this debate and if we are going to lose a lot of our younger people because of it.

- Our church did a two-year study on homosexuality because they took seriously what Annual Conference asked them to do. Too many churches have already made up their mind and aren't really seeking new information.

- What distresses me most about the way we deal with homosexuality is that people on both sides of the issue think that those who disagree are ignorant of Scripture and somehow inferior as Christians. I don't see how we can work our way through our differences when people are so disrespectful of those who disagree with them.

- Our name is still a problem. I was very bothered by the name when I joined the church. I felt like it needed to be changed, and I appreciated the fact that the [Womaen's] Caucus and others were working for a change. Part of the problem though is that the good

names are already taken. Most of the names people have come up with sound silly to me. But I'm telling you that people outside of our denomination hear the name and think we are like the Amish. And the name is offensive to some of our younger, well-educated women. I don't have the answer, but I think we need to deal with it.

- I love my local church, and I appreciate some of the district programs. I have more trouble with what's happening nationally. Why did the General Board push out the Andrew Center, On Earth Peace, the Association of Brethren Caregivers. . . ? Those things were all so valuable, and now we have all this increased competition for financial support. It's overwhelming for the local church to try and figure out how much to give to each organization. Are people really thinking through these decisions?

- We aren't willing to make tough decisions as a denomination. Look at all the years spent debating whether Elgin or New Windsor should be our main headquarters. We spent all that time and money, and we ended up coming up with reasons to continue to maintain both. I'm sorry, but we are too small to maintain both. We had staff who didn't want to move who influenced those decisions. At the district and local church level, we are never able to say "No" to a bad candidate for ministry. We have too many clergy who lack the skills that they need, and some of them hurt our churches. We need to have the courage to tell some people that God is calling them to something but it's not to being a local church pastor. I don't mean any of this to be hurtful, but I'm disappointed that the desire to please everyone keeps us from being realistic and healthy.

- We have to find ways to help people better share their faith and learn how to invite people to church. We have to learn how to make people feel welcome and how to integrate new people and long-time people into the church. That's the only way we're going to have a good future.

- I think the Church of the Brethren is the best-kept secret in a lot of communities. We offer the kind of warm, caring atmosphere for which people are hungry. We offer a setting that can help people grow closer to God. Most of the time we do a good job of living with our differences. What we don't do a good job of is telling people outside the church what we have to offer.

# Conclusions

There were interesting distinctions in what was emphasized in the different settings in which Together conversations took place. Some of those distinctions have been pointed out in the commentary on previous pages. While there were exceptions, for the most part:

- The emphasis on peace was most pronounced at district events, NOAC, and NYC. Congregations were less likely to comment at length on peace and were more likely to reflect some unease with the peace position of the denomination.

- People at NOAC, while very much aware of and valuing the past, were in fact among the most forward looking and the most open to change of any reporting.

- Teenagers at NYC shared the greatest appreciation for the church and also the greatest optimism over the future of the church.

- Congregations were the most likely to share concern about membership decline and fears about the future of the church and the denomination, though those concerns were also voiced in other settings.

There were relatively few differences on the basis of congregational size or region of the country. The theological tone of comments from the eastern and southern parts of the country was somewhat more conservative than in the midwestern and western regions. The hopes and concerns of participants, however, were very similar.

Comments from congregations served by pastors who were primarily trained outside the Church of the Brethren were more likely to reflect discomfort with the peace tradition, to reflect a very conservative approach to biblical interpretation, and to emphasize the importance of numerical growth. They were also less likely to talk about anointing and love feast. This strong correlation reminds us that pastors do have significant influence on their congregations, and that we need to be aware of such differences in perspective when licensing and ordaining for ministry.

As shared before, the structure of the Together discussions was designed to help people talk about the nature of the church and its future, not to discuss issues. It is significant, then, that some areas of difference still emerged. There were concerns about biblical interpretation, homosexuality, and decisions made at the national level of the denomination.

It appears that we need to find ways for continued discussion not only of our areas of agreement but also of our areas of difference. Our peace church tradition should lead us to a greater acceptance of differing opinions rather than to efforts to avoid conflict. One of the comments previously cited is especially insightful: "We need to recognize that the church is at times a place of conflict. **Christian life is a life in relationship**. . . . We won't always have harmony, and we need to show the ability to deal with conflicts" [emphasis added].

Indeed the Together process revealed, perhaps above all else, how much emphasis we place in our tradition on relationships—on our relationships with Jesus Christ and with each other. The acceptance and caring that we experience at the congregational level are part of the richness of our denomination. That emphasis on relationship and on faithfulness to Christ's call to care for all people draw us into service, and our focus on service is another of our rich denominational gifts.

One of our challenges for the future is to deepen our ability to tell others about our faith and about the kind of caring communities that our congregations offer. As one church observed, "The Church of the Brethren is the best-kept secret in a lot of communities. We offer the kind of warm, caring atmosphere for which people are hungry." The good news that we have received in the Church of the Brethren should not be kept a secret!

# Discussion guide

The questions that follow are designed for use in classes, groups, boards, and committees that want to explore the implications of the Together process for the congregation and the denomination. Enough questions are provided for at least two hours of discussion, but feel free to choose the questions of greatest interest if you have a shorter amount of time available.

1. Read 1 Corinthians 12:12-31. What do these verses say to you about the importance of the different gifts of people in the faith community? What do you think are the strongest gifts that you personally have for building up the body of Christ? What are the strongest gifts your congregation has? What are the strongest gifts we have as a denomination? What do these verses suggest about the way we respond to persons whose gifts for ministry are different than ours?

2. Did you participate in the Together conversations as an individual? Did your church participate in the Together conversations? If you were part of Together discussions, what did you find most helpful about them? If you did not participate, what, if anything, do you think you missed?

**3.** Pages 8-12 of this book offer ten different statements about the nature of the church. With which two statements do you most strongly identify? Why? With which two statements are you most uncomfortable? Why? Consider making a new statement as a group about the nature of the church.

**4.** Page 16 contains this statement: *"I've been a member for a decade now, and I still feel like a second-class citizen because I didn't grow up in the denomination, and I don't have a 'Brethren name.' People in our church just don't see you as having the same value if you came from another denomination and if you aren't related to someone they know."*

Have you ever felt that way yourself? Why, or why not? Would it be easy for someone in your congregation to feel that way? Why, or why not? How can people in the Christian community celebrate the gift of long-time relationships with others without causing some people to feel excluded or "second class"? How does Christ want us to respond to guests and to new members?

**5.** Which of the following do you consider core beliefs, values, or practices in the Church of the Brethren? Which should be viewed as optional?

What changes can be made in core beliefs, values, and practices without damaging our past and our future as a denomination?

- Love feast
- Feetwashing as a part of love feast
- Serving a full meal as a part of love feast
- Anointing
- Adult rather than infant baptism
- Baptism by immersion
- No creed
- The New Testament as our rule of faith and practice
- Being a peace church
- Avoiding internal conflict
- Taking public stands against war
- Working for peace in our communities
- An emphasis on service
- Brethren Volunteer Service
- Heifer International

6. Read Colossians 3:12-17. To what extent are these characteristics lived out in your local congregation? To what extent are they lived out within the Church of the Brethren as a denomination? Which of these are most important for the future of our church?

7. One person who participated in the Together process and read an early draft of this book made this statement: "We are becoming a denomination

with two distinct parts. One part is congregations and pastors who fully embrace the peace position of the denomination, who are actively engaged in service, who look at the Scriptures for guidance but do not take all verses literally, and who are willing to live with considerable diversity.

"The other part is congregations and pastors who do not buy into the peace emphasis, who take a very conservative look at the Scriptures, and who are not interested in much diversity—they want a creed that people must follow if they are to be good members."

To what extent do you agree or disagree with that categorization of pastors and churches? With which one of those "parts" would your congregation most closely identify? Why? In what ways are such categories an oversimplification?

8. While the Together process was not designed to examine issues, some areas of difference clearly came up. There were differing views on biblical interpretation, homosexuality, and what it means to be a peace church. Do you think our denomination would benefit from study in all our congregations on the topics that follow? Why, or why not?

   • How to use the Bible in daily life, and how to understand different approaches to the Bible

- How to relate our faith to our sexuality (talking not just about homosexuality but about what it means to be sexual persons created in God's image)

- What it means to be a peace church in our time

9. On page 34, there is a paragraph about differences in comments from churches served by pastors who were not primarily trained in the Church of the Brethren. How much influence does a pastor have on the beliefs and values of a congregation? Is it possible that some congregations intentionally seek a pastor who was trained outside of the denomination? Why, or why not? What is lost if pastors do not emphasize love feast, anointing, and the peace position of the denomination? Why is growth in membership an important concern for all congregations? What is the unique role of Bethany Theological Seminary and the Brethren Academy in our denomination?

10. Several participants expressed concern about the loss of membership at both the local church and the denominational levels over the past thirty years. What are factors that you think have contributed to the loss of members? What are some of the barriers to people more comfortably sharing their faith with others and inviting others to

church? What strategies would help reverse the membership decline?

11. Make a list of the "Top Ten Reasons for Belonging to Our Congregation." Identify the greatest strengths of your congregation. How can your church best interpret those strengths to the community and more effectively reach out to new people?

# To learn more

To explore the ministries, practices, and beliefs of the Church of the Brethren, visit **www.brethren.org**.

For additional reading, consider these and other books available at **www.brethrenpress.com** or by calling Brethren Press at 800-441-3712:

*Portrait of a People: The Church of the Brethren at 300,* by Carl Desportes Bowman

*Another Way of Believing: A Brethren Theology,* by Dale Brown

*Heart, Soul, and Mind: Becoming a Member of the Church of the Brethren* (a membership curriculum for youth and adults)

*Brethren During the Age of World War: The Church of the Brethren Encounter with Modernization, 1914-1950,* by Stephen L. Longenecker

*Fruit of the Vine: A History of the Brethren, 1708-1995,* by Donald F. Durnbaugh

# About the Together process

"Together: Conversations on Being the Church" was a process planned by a group of people who came together in 2003 to plan a way for the entire Church of the Brethren to engage in a conversation on what it means to be the church today. These people represented the Council of District Executives and all the agencies—the Association of Brethren Caregivers, Bethany Theological Seminary, Brethren Benefit Trust, General Board, and On Earth Peace—as well as the officers of Annual Conference. The project—including publication of this report—was made possible through special funding from these agencies.

Special thanks are due to those who gave time, energy, and prayerful support to plan the church-wide and district-wide conversations, those who served on Listening Teams, and the thousands who shared heart to heart in small groups with the intention of living ever more faithfully as the church of Jesus Christ.